Table of Contents

MATH 4

READING. 8

TEAMWORK. 12

COMMUNICATION. 16

STEM 23

LIFE SKILLS. 30

TEAM BUILDING. 36

INCENTIVES 40

About the Author

Alichia R. Parker is president and founder of A PAR Educational, LLC, an organization that enhances the learning ability of children through private tutoring, consulting, training, technical assistance and evaluation.

Creatively inclined, Alichia has developed a line of innovative educational games, <u>Multiplication Attack</u>, <u>Math Attack</u> and <u>Parts of Speech: Grammar Game</u>, with the goal of making learning fun and enjoyable.

In 2011, Ms. Parker founded the Malaika Learning Center, which boasts of serving over 100 children in preschool through 8th grade with educational programming which identifies, affirms and challenges each child's giftedness.

Alichia received her Bachelor of Arts degree in Elementary Education from Point Park University. She continued her education at the University of Pittsburgh in their Masters of Education program. There she successfully completed an internship and her coursework. Alichia has earned a Master of Science degree in Organizational Leadership from Geneva College.

"WHAT CHILDREN CAN DO WITH ASSISTANCE TODAY, THEY WILL BE ABLE TO DO BY THEMSELVES TOMORROW," is Alichia's heartfelt motto and her belief in teaching and instruction.

Alichia authored her first book, My Aunt and Me, in 2014.

From Alichia...

Wow! This Book has been a long time coming. I created many of these activities based on tutoring, training and professional development workshops that I have conducted over the years. It is an honor and privilege to serve children and youth, something that I have dedicated my life to. I strive to delight, inspire and develop people, pushing them to be as successful and effective as possible.

Throughout my journey as an educator, I have learned to meet my students where they are. I strive to serve youth with every activity of my life, teaching each child under my instruction, "Your success is my success!"

To the parents of the children that I have had the privilege and opportunity to work with, thank you for choosing me to shape and impact the life of your child.

I am proud to be an "Ambassador of Education."

Love,
Alichia R. Parker

MATH

Math Shred

Objective: Students use teamwork in order to solve a math word problem.

Type of Activity:
Math

Group Size:
4 players per group

Age Group:
9 & up

Materials:
- Shredded Math Word Problems
- Zip lock bags
- Chart Paper
- Markers
- Tape

Procedures:
1. Divide the students into teams of four.
2. Give each group an already shredded math word problem.
3. Explain to each group that they must take all of the shredded pieces and put them together.
4. Place each shredded piece in the correct sequence in order to create the math word problem.
5. After they read the word problem, the group must solve it.
6. Each group will write out their word problem with the correct answer on the chart paper.

Discussion Questions:
1. Was it easy or hard working with others to solve the problem?
2. How did you figure out the correct order of the pieces?
3. Did you feel valued and supported as a team member?

Soccer Ball Addition

Objective: Students will practice addition facts.

Type of Activity: Math

Group Size:
2 or more players

Age Group:
7 & up

Materials:
- Soccer Ball with numbers 0-12 written on it
- Music Player

Procedures:
1. Place chairs in a circle and have students stand in front of their chairs.
2. Turn on the music and ask students to pass the numbered soccer ball to each other without talking.
3. Whichever numbers the student's index fingers (pointer fingers) land on when catching the ball are the numbers they are to add together. For example, if one index finger lands on 7 and the other index finger lands on 3 the student says aloud "7+3=10."
4. Stop the music while the student adds the numbers together.
5. When finished, the student then passes the ball to someone else and the music begins again.
6. Students have to sit down if they get the problem wrong.
7. The last student standing wins.

Discussion Questions:
1. Was it challenging not being able to talk?
2. Can you describe how you felt when you had to add the two numbers quickly and accurately?
3. What did it feel like when you got the problem correct?

Numbers All Around Us

<u>Objective</u>: The students will be able to create subtraction math problems utilizing the numbers 1-12.

<u>Type of Activity</u>:
Math

<u>Group Size</u>:
1 or more

<u>Age Group</u>:
9 & up

Example 12-Square Grid

1	5	6	7
2	11	9	8
3	4	10	12

<u>Materials</u>:
- 4x6 piece of paper
- Pencils
- Timer

<u>Procedures</u>:
1. Allow the students to construct a 12 square grid on their piece of paper.
2. Students will choose 12 numbers 1-12 and write them in each square.
3. After they write the numbers in the squares they will be given two minus to come up with as many subtraction problems using the numbers in the grid (e.g., 11-4).
4. The students can only use a number one time.
5. The student who comes up with the most problems wins.

<u>Discussion Questions</u>:
1. What do you think would happen if you had more time?
2. Is there anther way to create more problems in the time given?
3. How important is it to know your math fact families?

Reading

Tongue Twister Fluency

<u>Objective</u>: The students will be able to practice fluency by using tongue twisters.

<u>Type of Activity:</u>
Reading

<u>Group Size</u>:
2 or more players

<u>Age Group:</u>
7 & up

<u>Materials</u>:
- Tongue Twister Sentences
- Timer

<u>Procedures</u>:
1. Divide students into groups of two.
2. Have students create a 5-7-word sentence tongue twister.
3. Each student will read the tongue twister and their partner must time their reading for 30 seconds.
4. The student who has the fastest time and the most words correct wins the activity.

<u>Discussion Questions:</u>
1. What process did you use to create your tongue twister?
2. How did time play a part in how well you read the sentences?
3. How easy or difficult was it to create your own tongue twisters?

Minute to Build It

Objective: Students will build as many words as possible within one minute.

Type of Activity:
Reading

Group Size:
2 or more players

Age Group:
7 & up

Materials:
- 1 set of consonant letter cards
- 2 sets of vowel cards (A, E, I, O, U, and Y)
- Dry erase board
- Dry erase markers
- One-minute timer

Procedures:
1. The students will break up into groups of two.
2. Each group will receive one set of consonant letter cards, two sets of vowel letter cards, dry erase board, dry erase markers and a one-minute timer.
3. One person will build the words with the assistance of his/her partner, and the partner will keep the time.
4. The person who is building the words will write the words on the dry erase board.
5. When one minute is up the partner will yell out "time's up."
6. Both participants will add up all the built words.
7. The team with the most words wins.

Discussion Questions:
1. What have you learned about working together?
2. How did you choose who would be the timekeeper and who would build the words?
3. How important was it to work together as a team?

Build a Word

Objective: The students will be able to participate in a word building activity utilizing letters of the alphabet.

Type of Activity:
Reading

Group Size:
2 or more players

Age Group:
7 & up

Materials:
- 2 set of consonant letter cards
- 2 sets of vowel cards (A, E, I, O, U, and Y)
- Timer

Procedures:
1. Divide the students into groups of two.
2. Pass out the index cards face down.
3. Give the students 3 minutes to build as many words as possible utilizing the cards given.
4. After the 3 minutes are up, each student should present their words to the group. The student with the most words...wins.

   Discussion Questions:
1. Was it challenging to use certain letters in the alphabet?
2. What letters of the alphabet did you use the most?
3. Could there be another way to build more words with less letters?

Teamwork

Wrap It Up

Objective: The students will use teamwork in order to transform teammates.

Type of Activity:
Teamwork

Group Size:
3 or more players

Age Group:
7 & up

Materials:
- 1 roll of toilet paper per team

Procedures:
1. Divide the students into groups of three to eight.
2. Give each team a roll of toilet paper.
3. Advise the teams that they have ten minutes to transform one team member into an agreed upon figure or thing by wrapping them in the provided toilet paper.
4. Encourage students to be creative by selecting a well-known figure like a doctor, firefighter, or a thing like a tree.
5. Once the teams are finished, each group must present their transformations.
6. Ask the most creative team to conduct a brief fashion show at the end of the activity.

Discussion Questions:
1. Tell me about your creation.
2. Was one roll of toilet paper enough to finish, or did you need more?
3. How did everyone feel about participating in the activity?

Act It Out

Objective: Students using teamwork to solve a problem.

Type of Activity:
Teamwork

Group Size:
4 or more players

Age Group:
9 & up

Materials:
- Common objects found in office, kitchen and or classroom

Procedures:
1. Divide the students into groups of four.
2. Allow the students to choose one object that they would like use as a prop. For example, an alarm clock, blender, microwave, chalkboard, etc.
3. The groups have ten minutes to plan a skit and utilize their chosen object as a prop in as many ways as possible.
4. Each time the prop is used the students will earn a point.
5. The group that earns the most points after performing their skit wins.

Discussion Questions:
1. What object did you use in order to involve everyone in the process of creating the skit?
2. How did you select your object to use for a prop?
3. If you could do something differently, what would it be?

Bombs Away

Objective: For students to utilize teamwork to complete a challenging task.

Type of Activity:
Teamwork

Group Size:
2 or more players

Age Group:
9 & up

Materials:
- String
- Bottle
- Pencils

Procedures:
1. Divide the students into groups of two.
2. Tie two pieces of string around the eraser end of a pencil.
3. Have two students stand back to back.
4. Tie the ends of the string around their waists so that the pencil is hanging down between them.
5. Place an empty bottle between the two students and challenge them to lower the pencil into the bottle without using their hands.
6. Allow several groups to go at once to see who can accomplish the task the fastest.

Discussion Questions:
1. What else could you have done in addition to tying the string around your waist?
2. Can you describe how you felt when you had to depend on your partner?
3. How did it feel not being able to use your hands?

Communication

Can You Build It?

Objective: The students will utilize communication skills to duplicate a model of building blocks.

Type of Activity:
Communication

Group Size:
4 or more players

Age Group:
12 & up

Materials:
- Building Blocks (such as LEGOS)
- Pictures of structures/objects
- Blindfolds
- Timer

Procedures:
1. Divide the students into teams of four.
2. Give each group a picture of a structure/object, bag of building blocks and a blindfold.
3. The group must choose a "builder."
4. Once they have identified a builder he/she must be blindfolded.
5. The other group members are shown the picture of the model to examine for two minutes.
6. After the two minutes are up, the picture is put away, the blindfold is removed from the builder, and he/she may begin building the model.
7. The builder must rely on the prompts from his/her teammates to recreate the picture using building blocks.
8. The other team members assist the builder by communicating what pieces go where until the model is built.

Discussion Questions:

1. How important was it for you as the builder to depend on your teammates for directives on how to build the LEGO model?
2. Would this have been easier if everyone was able to touch the blocks?
3. At any point during the activity, did you become frustrated?

Blind Fold Challenge

Objective: The students will be able to accomplish a challenging task only by utilizing verbal communication.

Type of Activity:
Communication

Group Size:
4 or more players

Age Group:
9 & up

Materials:
- A long string
- Blindfolds

Procedures:
1. Divide students into groups of four.
2. Blindfold everyone in the group and place the string with the ends tied together at the feet of the group members.
3. The students should stand shoulder to shoulder until the ends of the strings are tied together at their feet.
4. Challenge the group to form a shape out of the rope.
5. Once the group thinks it has created a perfect shape, allow everyone to take off their blindfolds and look at what they actually created.
6. Continue activity with different shapes such as triangles, circles and rectangles.

Discussion Questions:
1. What do you think would happen if you had one person giving directions on how to build a shape?
2. Is there another way to build a shape while being blindfolded?
3. Was it difficult having your feet tied together?

Do You Have It?

Objective: The students will be able to utilize communication skills to build a LEGO model.

Type of Activity
Communication

Group Size:
2 or more players

Age Group:
12 & up

Materials
- Building Blocks (like LEGOS)
- Note Cards
- Pencils

Procedures:
1. Divide the students into groups of two.
2. Give each group a pile of building blocks, note cards and writing instruments.
3. The teams will construct a LEGO model out of the building blocks.
4. Each team will write down step-by-step directions on how to duplicate the model.
5. After each group has constructed their model they must not let the other group see it.
6. After each group has compiled a complete set of directions, they must trade with another group to construct the model.
7. Each group will have 10 minutes to build the other group's model.
8. Lastly, have groups compare each model to the original for accuracy.

Discussion Questions:
1. Tell me about the steps you took to build a LEGO model?
2. What kind of information were you looking for while reading the other teams directions?
3. Would you do anything different to build a LEGO model?

Name That Gesture

Objective: Students will be able to work together as a team to practice communication skills.

Type of Activity
Communication

Group Size:
2 or more players

Age Group:
9 & up

Materials:
- Task Cards with gestures
- Timer

Procedures:
1. Divide students into groups of four.
2. Give students cards with tasks written on them such as, close the door, jump up and down, open the window, scratch your back, tie your shoe, crack your knuckles, etc.
3. One person will select the task card, but is not allowed to show anyone what it is.
4. Another person will have one minute to act out what is written on the task cards utilizing gestures, sounds and tones of voice.
5. The students cannot use direct words and or phrases.
6. The other members of the group will guess what the gesture is.
7. When the team guesses correctly they earn a point.
8. The group who has the most points after five rounds wins.

Discussion Questions:
1. Was this task easy or challenging?
2. How did it feel to utilize limited communication?
3. Would things have been different if you had more time to act out the gestures?

Name That Group

Objective: Students will work together to create a group story.

Type of Activity:
Communication

Group Size:
 3 or more players

Age Group:
9 & up

Materials:
- Paper
- Pencils

Procedures:
1. Divide the students into groups of three.
2. Give each group paper and a pencil.
3. Assign one group to another group.
4. Have each group write down all of the names of the people in their assigned group and then write a story about them.
5. When all the stories are finished, gather the groups back together.
6. Ask one person from each team to read their story, while their teammates act out the story.
7. Repeat this exercise for all teams.

Discussion Questions:
1. Was it easy or hard to come up with a story about your teammates?
2. How creative was your team with writing the story?
3. Were you distracting by the skit part of the story?

STEM

The Flying Ping Pong Ball

Objectives: Students will be able to work together as a team to launch a Ping-Pong ball.

Type of Activity:
STEM

Group Size:
3 or more players

Age Group:
   12 & up

Materials:
   - Ping Pong Ball
   - Small Paper Cups (3 oz.)
   - Duck Tape
   - Masking tape
   - Scissors
   - Cardstock
   - Jumbo Craft Sticks (6x11/16)
   - Definition Cars of a builder, architect, and spokesperson

Procedures:
   1. The students will gather all of the material that they will need to launch the Ping-Pong ball.
   2. The students will identify roles: a builder, architect and spokesperson.
   3. The students will have to construct an object out of the cardstock that will serve as a lever to launch the Ping-Pong ball.
   4. Once they have identified who is going to do what, they will brainstorm and identify what the model will look like.
   5. The architect will draw the model on paper and when he/she is finished, the architect will start designing the model with the input of the others.
   6. Once they are finished with the model, they will test it out to see if it works.
   7. When testing is complete, the spokesperson will present their model to the group.

Example Definition Cards:

Builder- The person who will build the object to launch the Ping-Pong ball.

Architect- The person who will draw what the model will look like.

Spokesperson- The person who will present their creation to the group.

Discussion Questions:

1. How important was it to rely on your teammates?
2. Would you explain how each person identified what their role would be (architect, builder, and spokesperson)?
3. What do you think would have happened if you did not work together as a team?

Pass the H2O

Objective: The students will be able to identify solutions for solving problems.

Type of Activity:
STEM

Group size:
4 or more players

Age Group
7 & up

Materials:
- Water
- Paper Cups
- Rubber Bands
- Scissors
- Paper Clips
- Construction Paper
- Tape

Procedures:
1. Divide the students into teams of four.
2. Give each team a cup full of water, rubber bands, scissors, paper clips, construction paper and tape.
3. Explain to each group that they must identify a Point A and a Point B.
4. Then direct the students to move the cup of water from Point A to point B without spilling any, any by only using the tools supplied to them.
5. No one is allowed to touch the cup of water with his or her hands at any point during the activity.

Discussion Questions:
1. Can you tell me how did you come up with a solution as a team?
2. What could you use to make it easier to get the water from point A to point B.
3. What do you think would happen if you were able to use your hands?

Eggs All Around Us

<u>Objective:</u> The students will be able to work together utilizing problem solving strategies.

<u>Type of Activity:</u>
STEM

<u>Group Size</u>:
4 or more players

<u>Age Group:</u>
9 & up

<u>Materials</u>:
- Raw eggs
- Tape
- String
- Drinking straws
- Paper
- Sticks
- Glue
- Paper clips

<u>Procedures</u>:
1. Divide the student into groups of four.
2. Give each team a raw egg and tell them that they must not allow their egg to break.
3. Instruct the groups to design a protective covering for their egg.
4. The groups can only use the materials provided to them.
5. Once their egg protectors are complete, groups will drop their eggs from at least four feet off of the ground, toss their egg back and forth a total of four times, and roll the egg across the table.
6. The groups whose egg survives intact...wins.

<u>Discussion Questions</u>:

1. How did your group choose to create your egg protector?
2. What was your greatest fear regarding this activity?
3. What strategy did you utilize so, that your egg would not break?

Stand Tall Activity

Objective: Students working together to complete a challenging task.

Type of Activity:
STEM

Group Size:
4 or more players

Age Group:
9 & up

Materials:
- Paper clips
- Paper
- Drinking straws
- Spaghetti noodles
- Paper cups
- Cookies
- Toothpicks
- Timers

Procedures:
1. Divide the students into groups of four.
2. Give each team a pile of materials and challenge them to build a tall tower.
3. They must build the tallest tower using the materials provided to them.
4. Allow them five minutes to complete this activity.
5. When the time has expired, permit each group to display their tower.

Discussion Questions:
1. What was challenging about this activity.
2. Could one person have done this project alone?
3. Would you explain how time played a factor in completing the goal?

Life Skills

I Know Who I Am

<u>Objective:</u> The students will be able to identify something that they learned about someone else.

<u>Type of Activity:</u>
Life Skills

<u>Group Size</u>:
2 or more players

<u>Age Group:</u>
7 & up

<u>Materials:</u>
- Blank Paper
- Pencils
- Timer

<u>Procedures:</u>
1. Distribute a blank piece of paper to the students.
2. Instruct them to write their names in the middle of the paper in all CAPITALIZED LETTERS with spacing in-between.
3. Tell the students they have five minutes to find someone and ask them two "getting to know you" questions.
4. Allow the students to move around the room and identify participants whose name fits the letters in their name.
5. When the student has identified a person whose name fits the letters in their name, ask that person two "getting to know you" questions. For example, how many siblings do you have? What's your favorite food?
6. Write an example on flip chart/chalkboard.
7. After they have identified that person they met than they will introduce the person, and what they have learned.

<u>Example:</u>   A L I C H I A
              L
              L
              E
              N

Discussion Questions:

1. Was it challenging to find someone whose name fit in with yours?
2. What did you learn about someone else?
3. Tell me did you have enough time to complete the activity?

Name That Tune

Objective: The students will be able to utilize listening and memorization skills.

Type of Activity:
Life Skills

Group Size:
2 or more players

Age Group:
5 & up

Materials:
- None

Procedures:
1. Ask a student to volunteer to hum or sing a song.
2. The student starts humming/singing a popular song.
3. The student who first recognizes the song earns a point.
4. If he/she can sing the next two or three lines of the song they earn another point.
5. Next, the student who recognized the song is the person who sings the next song.
6. The activity continues until one student earns ten points.

Discussion Questions:
1. Can you describe how you chose a song to hum/sing?
2. How did you feel when you earned a point?
3. How did you feel when you couldn't think of the words to the song?

Recipe for Success

Objective: For students to be able to identify characteristics of success.

Type of Activity:
Life Skills

Group Size:
2 or more

Age Group:
9 & up

Materials:
- Index Cards
- Pens

Procedures:
1. Give each student an index card and ask him or her to write down a recipe for success.
2. Explain to the students they will write on their index card just as they were reading a recipe. For example, 2 cups of education and information, 1 cup of love, ½ a cup of patience, 2 tablespoons of firmness, 1 tablespoon of creativity and 1 teaspoon of excitement and enthusiasm. Mix all of these ingredients together and stir into a pan. Place into the oven and bake for 45 minutes.
3. After everyone has created their own recipe, ask students to share their recipes.

Discussion Questions:
1. I'd be interesting in knowing what do you already know about success?
2. Will you try to follow the recipe you created?
3. Would you explain how you created your recipe?

Musical "I Spy"

Objective: The students will be able to verify specific objects that are a part of their environment.

Type of Activity:
Life Skills

Group Size:
2 or more players

Age Group:
5 & up

Materials:
- Music Player

Procedures:
1. Ask the students to pick a number from 1-10. The student who chooses the correct number becomes the spy.
2. The students who are not the spy will put their heads down and close their eyes.
3. Play music while the spy is looking for something to identify. Stop the music when the spy says "I spy _BLANK_ with my natural eye."
4. Optional: The spy can provide hints while the students are guessing.
5. The students will lift their heads up and guess what the spy has noticed.
6. Once the student has guessed what the spy has noticed than that student will become the spy.
7. The game will continue until time allows or the facilitator/leader senses the students are ready to transition.

Discussion Questions:
1. What important lesson have you learned just by keeping your head down?
2. Can you describe how easy/hard it was to choose an object that was a part of the environment?
3. How important is patience while listening to the spy?

Team Building

The Highest Tower

Objective: Students will work together as a group to build a card tower.

Type of Activity:
Team Building

Group Size:
2 or more players

Age Group:
9 & up

Materials:
- One deck of playing cards per team
- Timer

Procedures:
1. Divide the students into teams of two or four.
2. Give each team a deck of cards.
3. Instruct the teams to build card towers as high as possible within ten minutes.
4. Each student can only use one hand to build.
5. Have students place their free hand behind their backs.
6. Teams must start over whenever the tower falls.
7. Once the timer goes off, allow the teams to identify who has the tallest card tower.

Discussion Questions:
1. How frustrated did you get during this activity?
2. Could you have come up with alternate ways to build a tower if you could use both of your hands?
3. What kind of information did you need to accomplish this task?

Backs Against the Wall

Objective: The students will be able to work together to formulate a plan.

Type of Activity:
Team Building

Group Size:
2 or more players

Age Group:
9 & up

Materials: None

Procedures:
1. Divide the students into teams of two.
2. Challenge students to sit down on the floor Indian style with their backs firmly against one another.
3. Have them lock elbows and attempt to stand up without unlocking arms.
4. Once a team successfully stands up, they need to find another team that has been successful and form a larger group.
5. Once they have found the other group, they must sit back down on the floor, back to back and attempt to stand up all together.

Discussion Questions:
1. What strategy did you come up with as a team to accomplish this goal?
2. Was it easier for you to sit down as a group or to stand up as a group?
3. Is there another way to stand up without using your arms?

Name That Group Activity

Objective: The students will be able to work together to create a group story.

Type of Activity:
Team Building

Group Size:
3 or more

Age Group:
7 & up

Materials:
- Paper
- Pencils

Procedures:
1. Divide the students into groups of three.
2. Give each group paper and a pencil.
3. Assign each group to another group.
4. Have them write down all of the names of the people in that group and then write a story about them.
5. When all the stories are finished, gather the groups back together.
6. Ask one person from each team to read their story, while the person is reading the story the other group members should be acting out the story.
7. Repeal for all groups.

Discussion Questions:
1. Do you think it was easy or hard to come up with a story about your teammates?
2. How creative was your team with writing the story?
3. Did the skit distract you, and if so, in what way?

Incentives

Incentives...

are important in reinforcing positive outcomes and they do not have to break the bank.

Below are a few suggested rewards for hard work.

- Favorite snacks and candy
- Small items from your local dollar store that can be placed into a treasure box for students to pick from
- A special role/job for the day...like being a class helper
- Affirmation and praise
- Stickers
- Create a "wall of winners" and allow students to add their names
- Small homemade trophy
- Take a picture of the student and hang it as "the winner of the day/week"
- Print a certificate
- Give extra credit points
- Free/Late homework pass
- Homework free weekend
- Extended recess
- Popcorn or Ice cream party
- Call to parents with positive comments

www.ingramcontent.com/pod-product-compliance
Lightning Source LLC
Chambersburg PA
CBHW081305040426
42452CB00014B/2664